GREECE
the land

Sierra Adare

A Bobbie Kalman Book

The Lands, Peoples, and Cultures Series

 Crabtree Publishing Company
www.crabtreebooks.com

The Lands, Peoples, and Cultures Series

Created by Bobbie Kalman

Coordinating editor
Ellen Rodger
Proofreader: Adrianna Morganelli

Editors
Virginia Mainprize
Greg Nickles
Ellen Rodger

Project development, writing, and design
Water Buffalo Books
Mark Sachner
Sabine Beaupré
MaryLee Knowlton

Revisions and Updates
Plan B Book Packagers
Redbud Editorial

Special thanks to
The Greek Tourism Office and Office of the
Minister of Business, New York; Gonda Van Steen,
Department of Classics, University of Arizona; the
Panos family, Marsha Baddeley

Photographs
Cornel Achirei/Shutterstock, Inc.: cover, p. 31 top;
Archive/Photo Researchers: page 16; Frederick
Ayer/Photo Researchers: p. 7; Jeff
Banke/Shutterstock, Inc.: p. 8; Clement K.L.
Cheah/Shutterstock, Inc.: p. 18 (top), p. 29; Paul
Cowan/Shutterstock, Inc.: p. 26 (top); Marc
Crabtree: p. 30; easyshoot/Shutterstock, Inc.: p. 30
(top); Margot Granitsas/Photo Researchers: p. 24 (top); Wolfgang
Kaehler: p. 3, p. 10, p. 12, p. 13, p. 26 (bottom),
 p. 27, p. 30 (bottom); Andreas G. Karelias/Shutterstock, Inc.: p. 23
(bottom); Noboru Komine/Photo Researchers: p. 21 (top);
Francois Le Diascorn/Photo Researchers: p. 24 (bottom); Eva
Madrazo/Shutterstock, Inc.: p. 18 (bottom); Palis
Michael/Shutterstock, Inc.: p. 19 (top), p. 25 (top); Martina
Misar/Shutterstock, Inc.: p. 28; Ioannis Papadimitriou
/Shutterstock, Inc.: p. 4; paradoks_blizanaca/Shutterstock, Inc.:
p. 1; Porterfield/Chickering/Photo Rsearchers: p. 24 (bottom); Carl
Purcell: p. 15; Styve Reineck/Shutterstock, Inc.: p. 17; David
H.Seymour/Shutterstock, Inc.: p. 22; Fedor A. Sidorov
/Shutterstock, Inc.: p. 19 (bottom); Petros Tsonis/Shutterstock, Inc.:
p. 20; Zdorov Kirill Vladimirovich/Shutterstock, Inc.: p. 9;
Vanni/Art Resource, NY: p. 14; Maria Yfanti/Shutterstock, Inc.:
p. 23 (top)

Illustrations
Susan Tolonen: pages 10–11, back cover
Jim Chernishenko: map p. 5

Cover
The Greek Orthodox church at Oia, Santorini, is famous for its
white walls and blue domed roof whose color matches that of
the sea.

Title page
Greece is known for its sunny climate and many islands on the
Aegean Sea and Ionian Sea.

Back cover
An ancient vase depicts men harvesting olives from an olive tree.

Library and Archives Canada Cataloguing in Publication

Adare, Sierra
    Greece : the land / Sierra Adare.

(Lands, peoples, and cultures series)
Includes index.
ISBN 978-0-7787-9308-3 (bound).--ISBN 978-0-7787-9676-3 (pbk.)

    1. Greece--Description and travel--Juvenile literature.
2. Greece--History--Juvenile literature. I. Title. II. Series.

DF717.A32 2007   j949.5   C2007-906215-6

Library of Congress Cataloging-in-Publication Data

Adare, Sierra.
    Greece. the land / Sierra Adare. -- [Rev. ed.].
        p. cm. -- (Lands, peoples, and cultures)
    Includes index.
    ISBN-13: 978-0-7787-9308-3 (rlb)
    ISBN-10: 0-7787-9308-7 (rlb)
    ISBN-13: 978-0-7787-9676-3 (pb)
    ISBN-10: 0-7787-9676-0 (pb)
    1. Greece--Description and travel--Juvenile literature. 2. Greece--History--Juvenile
literature. I. Title. II. Series.

DF728.A33 2007
914.5--dc22   2007041636

Crabtree Publishing Company

www.crabtreebooks.com   1-800-387-7650
Copyright © **2008 CRABTREE PUBLISHING COMPANY.** All rights reserved. No part of this publication may be reproduced, stored in a retrieval
system or be transmitted in any form or by any means, electronic, mechanical, photocopying, recording, or otherwise, without the prior written permission
of Crabtree Publishing Company. In Canada: We acknowledge the financial support of the Government of Canada through the Book Publishing Industry
Development Program (BPIDP) for our publishing activities.

Published in Canada
Crabtree Publishing
616 Welland Ave.
St. Catharines, ON
L2M 5V6

Published in the United States
Crabtree Publishing
PMB16A
350 Fifth Ave., Suite 3308
New York, NY 10118

Published in the United Kingdom
Crabtree Publishing
White Cross Mills
High Town, Lancaster
LA1 4XS

Published in Australia
Crabtree Publishing
386 Mt. Alexander Rd.
Ascot Vale (Melbourne)
VIC 3032

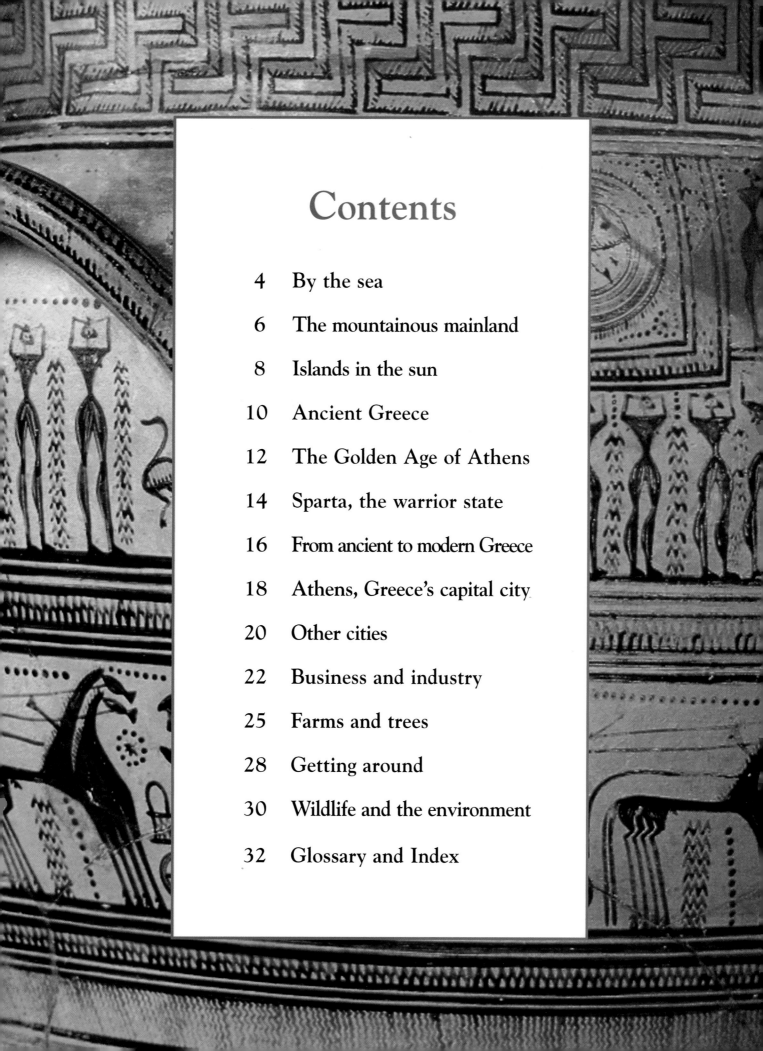

Contents

By the sea

Few nations have contributed as much to world culture as Greece. Many of our ideas about government, medicine, **architecture**, sports, literature, art, mathematics, law, and **astronomy** have roots that go back thousands of years to ancient Greece. Many of the subjects studied in school today were first taught in ancient Greece. The Greece of today is different from ancient Greece. After centuries of being controlled by other nations, Greece has been an **independent** country since 1830. Despite differences between ancient and modern Greece, much of the land has remained as it was centuries ago.

The lure of the sea

For thousands of years, the sea has played an important role in the lives of the Greek people. Even today, many Greeks earn their living from the sea, some by fishing and others by shipping materials from all over the world. The sea also attracts tourists who visit Greece's beautiful beaches and bask in its sunny climate.

(opposite) Santorini, in the Cyclades, is a group of volcanic islands in the Aegean Sea. Santorini is a popular tourist destination.

Wherever you travel in mainland Greece, mountains are not far away. Over three-quarters of Greece is covered with mountains. The Pindus range runs down the middle of the country, and the Olympus range lies along the east coast. In most places, the soil is thin and rocky, but between the mountains, in central and northern Greece, lie two large, fertile plains. Mountains divide the mainland of Greece into six main regions, called provinces: Thrace, Macedonia, Thessaly, Epirus, Central Greece, and Peloponnese.

Traditional Thrace

Thrace, in northeastern Greece, is a small province that borders Bulgaria and Turkey. Until 1923, Thrace was part of Turkey, and even today it feels and looks more like Turkey than Greece. Traditional Turkish-style baggy pants, full shirts, and headdresses are sometimes still worn by villagers. Tobacco, the province's largest crop, is grown in the valleys and on the plains.

Macedonia, the largest province

To the west of Thrace lies Macedonia. This province was once a part of the ancient kingdom of Macedonia, and it shares a border with the Republic of Macedonia, an independent country to the north of Greece. The province of Macedonia also borders Albania and Bulgaria. The province's continental climate brings cold winters and warm summers. Cotton and rice are grown in the huge plain that lies in the middle of the province. The rest of the land is mainly mountainous, and the slopes of Mount Vermio are a center for winter sports.

(above) A monastery built on the top of a rock formation seems to rise out of Greece's mountainous landscape.

(opposite page) The peninsula *of Peloponnese is divided from the mainland by the Corinth Canal, completed in 1893.*

6

Thessaly, Greece's breadbasket

Thessaly, in central Greece, is surrounded by high mountain peaks. Summers in this province are very hot, and winters are cold and damp. Thessaly is called "the breadbasket of Greece" because grain is grown on the fertile plain that lies in the center of the province. Thessaly is also famous for its olives.

Epirus, the mountainous region

Epirus, which lies in the northwest corner of Greece, has majestic mountains and deep valleys. The Pindus Mountains isolate the province from the rest of mainland Greece. Shepherds still wander through mountain pastures with their flocks of sheep and goats.

Sunny Central Greece

Most of Central Greece is made up of low hills and plains covered with vineyards, olive groves, and orchards. The climate is milder than in the northern provinces. Part of Central Greece, named Attica, is called "the heart of Greece" because it contains Greece's capital city, Athens, and Piraeus, a busy port. To the east, lies the large island of Euboia, which is connected to the mainland by a bridge.

Peloponnese, the giant to the south

Many of Greece's mountain ranges form long strips of land that reach into the sea as peninsulas. Greece's most southern province, Peloponnese, is a vast and mountainous peninsula of high peaks and coastal plains. The region's sunny climate, with hot, dry summers and mild winters, has made it famous for the citrus fruits and early-harvest vegetables it **exports** to the rest of Europe. Grain fields and olive groves dot the landscape. Small villages are found in sheltered bays along the coast. Higher up in the mountains, stone houses sit on narrow ledges of bare, gray rock cliffs.

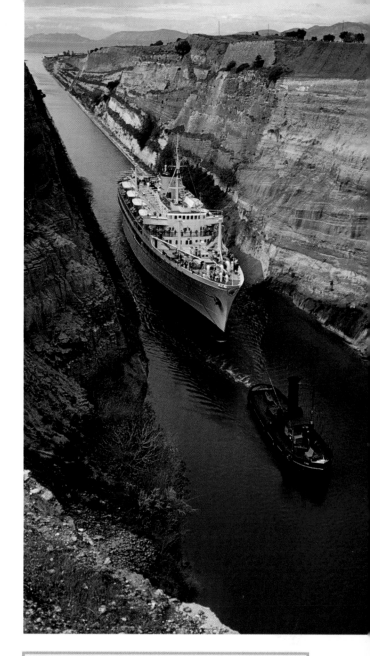

Earthquake!

Greece sits on the Balkan Peninsula, which occasionally shakes with earthquakes and milder earth tremors. Ancient Greeks believed earthquakes were caused by angry Poseidon, the god of the sea. A well-known earthquake was reported in the ninth century A.D. This quake destroyed Corinth and may have killed as many as 45,000 people. In 1999, an earthquake centered near Athens, destroyed buildings and killed about 100 people. Newer Greek buildings are built to be safe from tremors.

In addition to their golden beaches and rocky terrain, the islands of the Cyclades are known for their blue skies and windmills.

Greece's more than 1,400 islands are actually the tops of undersea mountain ranges. The islands make up one-fifth of Greece's total land area, but fewer than 200 islands are inhabited. The largest Greek island is Crete. The other islands are divided into five groups: the Sporades, Ionian, Cyclades, Dodecanese, and Northeastern Aegean islands.

The Sporades

The Sporades islands, which run east of the coast of Thessaly, are known for their fresh seafood, bright sunshine, lush forests, jagged coastlines, and pleasant temperatures. These islands are actually extensions of Mount Pelion, on a peninsula in Thessaly.

The Ionians

The Ionian islands form a chain from Peloponnese up along the western coast of Greece. Corfu, the most northern and best known of these islands, lies about two miles (three kilometers) off the coast of Albania.

The Cyclades

Spread out southeast of Athens in the central and southern Aegean Sea, the Cyclades were named by ancient Greeks for the circular, or cyclical, pattern that they form around the holy island of Delos. The tiniest island of the group, Delos was, according to the ancient Greeks, the birthplace of the god Apollo and his twin sister, Artemis. Today, Delos is one large **archaeological** site, and most of its **inhabitants** are people who work at the island's museum and ancient ruins.

The Dodecanese

East of the Cyclades are the Dodecanese, which means "twelve islands" in Greek. The Dodecanese actually have more than twelve islands if you count several smaller ones. The Dodecanese are closer to southwestern Turkey than to the mainland of Greece. Like the Cyclades, they have hot summers and mild winters. Rhodes, the largest and most famous island in the chain, is called the island of the sun. Most Greeks on these islands earn their living from the sea and tourism.

The Northeast Aegeans

The Northeast Aegean islands are scattered throughout the Aegean Sea. Fishing villages along the coasts give way to inland vineyards, olive groves, and pine forests. While tourism has changed many islanders' way of life, wine production, olive growing, and lumbering are still important ways of earning a living.

Crete

Crete's snowcapped mountains rise with breathtaking beauty above its plains and coast. A deep gorge, the largest in Europe, splits Crete's western plain. The largest of the Greek islands, Crete is the site of Europe's oldest civilization, the Minoan civilization, which dates back 5,000 years and flourished from 1700 B.C. to 1400 B.C.

Today, Crete has mountain villages, farmland, and modern cities. Many people consider its climate the mildest and healthiest in all of Europe. Winds from the north blow hot and dry during the summer, especially in the interior of the island, where the cool sea breezes are not felt. During the winter, the winds bring rain and cooler temperatures.

Flat-roofed houses are clustered on a hill in a small mountain village on the island of Crete.

Ancient Greece

Archaeologists have discovered that during prehistoric times, before written history, wandering groups of people roamed through what is today Greece and eventually settled into communities. Some of these communities grew into large and powerful empires.

The Minoan civilization

The first great kingdom developed on the island of Crete. Ruled by King Minos, the people were known as the Minoans. They built the palace of Knossos around 1700 B.C. It was no ordinary palace. It contained more than 1,000 rooms surrounding a courtyard. The queen enjoyed such luxuries as a flush toilet and a bath with running water!

The Mycenaeans

Mycenae was a rich and powerful state that dominated Greece from about 1600 to 1200 B.C. It was named after its fortress city, Mycenae, in the Peloponnese. The Mycenaean civilization, with its warrior kings, was destroyed by the Dorians, Greek-speaking invaders from the north.

The rise of the city-states

Towns in ancient Greece were separated by mountains. This isolation led to the growth of the city-state, or *polis*, around 800 B.C. Independent city-states grew up around an *acropolis*, the highest point in the area, such as a hill or plateau. City-states also had fortresses, called citadels, farms, houses, and a market, or agora, in the center of the city.

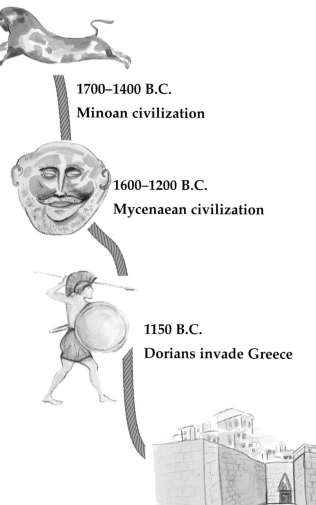

1700–1400 B.C.
Minoan civilization

1600–1200 B.C.
Mycenaean civilization

1150 B.C.
Dorians invade Greece

800 B.C.
Rise of the Greek city-states

The agora was surrounded by public buildings, such as the *bouleuterion*, or council hall, a sports stadium, and temples dedicated to Greek gods and goddesses. Each city-state had its own ruler and government, its own religious traditions, legends, and sporting events. Each city-state grew its own crops and traded with other city-states. Two of the most powerful city-states were Athens and Sparta.

(opposite page) A painting of women in blue on the wall of the palace of Knossos, a magnificent structure built on Crete by the ancient Minoans.

The battle of Marathon

In 490 B.C., Persia, a mighty empire in the east, attacked the city-state of Athens. A fleet of Persian ships crossed the Aegean Sea, and 20,000 archers and **cavalry** landed near Athens on the Plain of Marathon. The much smaller Athenian army was waiting for them. For eight days a fierce battle raged, until the Persians were defeated. The Athenian general sent a messenger to Athens. The messenger ran 25 miles (40 kilometers) without stopping, announced the victory, and dropped dead. This event inspired the marathon race.

750–550 B.C.
Greek expansion into other territories (Europe, Asia, and North Africa)

477–405 B.C.
Golden Age of Athens

490–479 B.C.
Persian Wars

431–404 B.C.
Peloponnesian Wars

776 B.C.
First Olympic games

336 B.C.
Alexander the Great

CXLVI

146 B.C.
Roman rule

1830
Greek independence

A.D. 1453–1829
Turkish Ottoman Empire

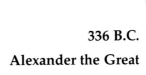

A.D. 330–1453
Byzantine Empire

The Golden Age of Athens

Overlooking the city of Athens from the Acropolis is the Parthenon, a temple that still commands the awe of both residents and tourists. Today, Athenians are concerned with preserving the Parthenon and its unique architecture, such as the porch shown here.

Ancient Greece was dominated by two city-states, Athens and Sparta. They were very different from each other, but both played an important role in the ancient Greek world. After Athens defeated the Persian army, the city enjoyed a period of peace and prosperity known as the Golden Age of Athens.

A center for the arts

Athens was named after Athena, the goddess of wisdom, arts, and crafts. The city became a center for arts, science, and literature. It was home to some of the greatest poets, playwrights, **philosophers**, and political leaders in history. Local artisans created fine pottery and jewelry. Architects designed magnificent public buildings and temples filled with bronze, gold, or marble statues of Greek heroes, gods, and goddesses. During the period of peace that followed the war with Persia, Athens built some of its finest buildings, including the Parthenon, a magnificent temple on top of the Acropolis.

Athenian government

Athens was a democracy, which means that the citizens elected their leaders. Every nine days, the *ekklesia*, or elected assembly, met in the agora to pass laws and make decisions. Any native-born Athenian male who was not a slave, was considered a citizen and could stand up and speak in the assembly. After all who wished to speak had their say, the discussions ended, and the members of the assembly voted.

Who were the citizens of Athens?

Only free males could choose their leaders and vote. Women, slaves, and former slaves were not considered citizens and could not vote. Slaves who showed exceptional bravery on the battlefield were sometimes given their freedom and Athenian citizenship.

Daily life

Early each morning, the agora, or marketplace, began to fill up with the male citizens of Athens. Businessmen, on their way to work, stopped for a chat. Tradesmen opened their shops or set up stalls selling meat, fish, cheese, and vegetables, wine, pottery, and **textiles**.

Women spent most of their time at home. They lived in a separate section of the house. They planned the meals and wove cloth for the family's clothes, but often slaves did the cleaning, shopping, and most of the cooking.

After sunset, the men came home for the main meal. Wealthy men often entertained their friends in the evening. They lay on couches, listening to music and poetry, enjoying the food and wine served to them by their slaves.

Modern Athens has spread out around the Acropolis, the center of ancient Athens.

Slavery

Every Greek city-state had its slaves—men, women, and children captured in war and sold by slave traders in the agora. Slaves cooked, cleaned, and looked after small children. They worked in mines and small factories and on farms. Slaves had no political rights and could not vote.

Sparta, the warrior state

The other important Greek city-state was Sparta. Spartan citizens were forbidden to work. They depended entirely on *helots*, land slaves who worked on the farms. Because the Spartans were always afraid the *helots* would revolt, they developed a strong warrior society.

Little culture

Sparta was little more than a collection of wooden houses and farms. It had no magnificent temples, and its people produced few works of art or literature. Today, only a few Spartan ruins remain. They lie outside the modern Greek city of Sparta, in the southeast Peloponnese.

A soldier's life

Every young male citizen of Sparta served as a full-time soldier, called a *hoplite*. He wore a bronze helmet, an armored breastplate, leggings, and a red cloak. He carried a shield, a spear, and sometimes swords or bows and arrows. *Hoplites* were a fearsome sight as they marched against Sparta's enemies.

In ancient Sparta, children did not belong to their parents but to the state. State officials examined every newborn, and if the baby was sick or weak, it was left to die in the mountains. At the age of seven, boys were taken from their families to live in military barracks, where they stayed until they were 30. They were trained for war and taught discipline.

As spartan as a Spartan

Sparta was a warrior society that produced the best soldiers in ancient Greece. The ancient city-state has left one important reminder of its past: the word spartan, which describes someone who shows discipline and courage. It also describes something that is simple, rugged, or without decoration, such as a spartan lifestyle, a spartan room, or a spartan diet.

This carving of a Spartan warrior was made around 490 B.C.

They received only one tunic to wear for the entire year. Young boys were whipped to teach them to accept pain. Some let themselves be whipped to death to show their bravery. If a young soldier broke any rules, he lost his citizenship and the right to own slaves. He was forced to wear special clothing that identified his crime.

Girls and women

Spartan girls had more freedom than other girls in ancient Greece. They exercised and wore short tunics that allowed them to run freely. The state wanted girls to be strong so they would grow up to become mothers of warriors. Like women in other city-states, Spartan women could not vote or hold positions of power.

Sparta valued security more than personal freedom. It did not have a democratic government and was ruled by kings. Anyone who broke the law or spoke out against the government or its rules could be put to death.

Sparta's power

Sparta was at the height of its power between the eighth and fourth centuries B.C. In 431 B.C., Sparta, wanting to end the growing influence of its rival city-state, went to war with Athens. This conflict led to a series of land and sea battles, known as the Peloponnesian Wars. In 404 B.C., Sparta defeated Athens. Years of war had weakened all the Greek city-states, however, and they became easy targets for invaders from the north – the Macedonians.

Sparta today is a quiet town in southern Greece.

In 338 B.C., a Macedonian king, Philip II, invaded Greece, bringing many of the city-states under his control. In 336 B.C., Philip was **assassinated**. His twenty-year-old son Alexander became king of Macedonia and ruler of Greece.

Alexander the Great

Alexander was a military genius who never lost a battle. In the three years after he became king, Alexander conquered the rest of Greece. With a combined Greek and Macedonian army, he defeated the Persian empire. Leading his troops east, Alexander conquered every army he met along the way, until he reached India. His soldiers refused to go further, so Alexander turned around and led his tired army home. Alexander died of fever at 32, after he had created the largest empire in the world.

The Romans

After Alexander died, his generals fought each other and divided his lands. The empire was never so powerful as it had been under Alexander. It was conquered by Rome, a mighty civilization to the west. In 146 B.C., Greece became a Roman province. Like Alexander, the Romans admired all things Greek and spread Greek culture to other parts of the world.

The Byzantine Empire

In 330 A.D., the Roman emperor Constantine moved the capital of the empire from Rome to the ancient Greek city of Byzantium, in what is today Turkey. He renamed the city Constantinople. After Constantine's death, the Roman empire was divided, and Constantinople remained the capital of the eastern part. For 1,000 years, this Byzantine empire remained Greek-speaking. In 1453, the Ottomans, or Turks, captured Constantinople and took control of all the empire, including Greece.

Independence

Greece remained a part of the Turkish empire for nearly 400 years, but Greeks dreamed of ruling their own country. In 1821, they revolted against the Turks in a war of independence. In 1830, Greece became an independent country. Today, Greece is a democratic republic, with a premier and an elected parliament.

Alexander the Great spread Greek ideas and culture throughout his vast empire.

In Athens, a guard watches over a memorial to those who lost their lives fighting for modern Greece.

17

In the 1830s, following independence from Turkish rule, Athens was still a small village of about 4,000 people. Gathered beneath the Acropolis were a jumble of small wooden huts, crumbling ruins, and a maze of dirt alleys. Since then, Athens has grown tremendously. Today, eight million people live in Athens and its metropolitan area. Visitors are often surprised to find a huge, sprawling, modern city filled with noise, constant traffic, and crowds of people.

Reminders of the past

High atop the Acropolis sits the Parthenon, the magnificent temple built in the fifth century B.C. Around the city and its suburbs are many other reminders of the city's ancient Greek, Roman, and Turkish past.

The "urban monster"

Seeking a better life, people pour into the "urban monster," as Athens has been called, from rural areas. City housing, roads, and utilities have been unable to keep up with the population growth. Possibly most serious of all Athens' big-city problems is air pollution, the result of too many cars. To reduce traffic, Athens is constantly extending its underground rail system and has created areas where no cars are allowed.

(right) A freshly butchered chicken hangs outside a butcher shop in Athens.

(above) Modern shops and apartments line the streets of Athens on a backdrop of ancient ruins.

A modern city

Athens is like other modern cities, but with a style of its own. Fast food and pizza restaurants share business with the **tavernas**, the traditional places where Greeks gather to talk, eat, drink, and enjoy music. Athens is a city that never sleeps, especially in the city center. Day and night the streets are filled with traffic. People are still chatting on street corners or walking home from cafés just before dawn.

(right) The subway system in Athens is called the Attiko Metro. Some subway stations are mini museums that house ancient artifacts found during subway line construction.

(below) Athens sprawls out on several hills.

19

Other cities

Thessaloniki

The port of Thessaloniki, Greece's second largest city, was founded in 315 B.C. by a Macedonian general who named it after his wife, the sister of Alexander the Great. Today, Roman ruins, Byzantine churches, and Turkish buildings stand out among the city's modern high rises. Although it is no longer white, the 500-year-old White Tower is one of the city's most famous landmarks. It was used as a prison by the Turks.

Pátras, the great seaport

A major port in the Peloponnese and Greece's third largest city, Pátras is a transportation hub. The city is also an important industrial center and university town. It has a lively carnival season, a summer festival season, and many places to eat and socialize.

Ioánnina, Ali Pasha's fortress

Ioánnina, which stands on the edge of a large lake in a wide, green valley, is known as the city of Ali Pasha. In 1788, Ali was appointed pasha, or ruler, of the region by the Turks. When he became too powerful, they sent an army of 50,000 soldiers to surround the city. Ali offered to sign a deal with the Turks, but when he arrived at the meeting place, he found a firing squad waiting for him. Today, Ioánnina is a modern commercial and university city. It has several old mosques dating from Turkish rule.

The Rio-Antirio bridge in Pátras is the largest cable-stayed bridge in the world.

Rhodes: an ancient capital

The city of Rhodes, for over 2,000 years the capital of the island of Rhodes, is now a popular tourist resort. It is situated on the northeastern corner of the island of Rhodes, facing the coast of Turkey. Ancient Rhodes was known for its colossus, an enormous statue of the god Helios. Modern Rhodes is a city divided into two sections: the Old Town and the New Town. Old Town, surrounded by fortress walls built 600 years ago, is a maze of narrow cobblestone lanes that lead to many reminders of the city's past. New Town is a modern district with hotels, fast food restaurants, and entertainment centers. The economy of Rhodes is based on tourism and many tourists come to see the island's historic sites.

Inside the walls of Old Town are many reminders of Rhodes's past: ancient Greek ruins, Byzantine churches, Turkish mosques, and a restored Jewish synagogue. People can go for steam baths at some of the city's magnificent Turkish baths. Built in the 1400s, they still work!

The Colossus of Rhodes

According to tradition, the Colossus was a huge bronze statue of the sun god Helios, 98 feet (30 meters) high. It is usually shown standing over the harbor of Rhodes, with a foot on each shore and ships passing between its legs. Most historians feel that it probably stood beside the harbor, not above it, however. The Colossus, one of the Seven Wonders of the Ancient World, was toppled by an earthquake in 225 B.C. Small copies of the Colussus are sold in souvenir shops all over the island.

 # Business and industry

Greeks like to run their own businesses. Most of the non-farming work force is employed by small, family-owned businesses often based on the tourist trade, such as shops and cafés. The rest of the labor force works in industries, such as shipping, mining, manufacturing, and food processing.

Tourism: a big business in Greece

One of the largest sources of income in Greece today is tourism. Tourists from all over the world travel to Greece to see its ancient buildings and archaeological sites. In the summer, they flock to Greece's beaches and seaside resorts. A new trend, ecotourism, gives tourists activities that have a low impact on the natural environment.

Ecotourism provides undeveloped areas to hike and bike in national forests and parks. Some people, however, would like to see more mountain forests cleared for ski resorts and hotels.

Shipping and shipbuilding

Since ancient times, Greeks have built and sailed ships. Today, Greece is known for its fleet of merchant ships, the third largest in the world. Large freighters carry goods from country to country. The Greeks also own many shipyards, where ships are repaired and new ones are built.

The Corinth Canal promotes shipping by connecting the Gulf of Corinth with the Aegean Sea.

Mining natural resources

Greece mines several natural resources. Most of them are exported to other nations for processing. Bauxite and lignite are two of Greece's most important mineral resources. Bauxite, a claylike material, is the main ore in aluminum. Lignite is a brownish-black soft coal that has a slightly woody texture. Greece also produces magnesium, a silver-white metallic **element** that burns with a brilliant white flame. It is used for the flash in cameras and to set off fireworks and bombs. For centuries, Greece has been known for its marble, a limestone that can be polished and used in buildings and statues.

From farm to factory

Most manufacturing in Greece is based on the use of farm products such as cotton, which is grown for clothing, manufacturing tobacco products, canning fruit, and winemaking. Industrial production has grown in recent years. Factories manufacture metal products, rubber, plastics, and electrical machinery. Most of the larger factories are near the nation's two biggest cities, Athens and Thessaloniki.

(above) A tourist boat designed to look like one from Greek mythology. Tourism is a major industry in Greece.

(below) An industrial dockyard in Pireaus.

23

A smaller catch

Many foreigners think of fishing as *the* Greek occupation. After all, Greece has a strong maritime tradition, a thriving shipbuilding industry, a long and winding coastline, and over 1,400 islands.

While fishing is an important economic activity, pollution and the overfishing of coastal waters have hurt the fishing industry. As a result, fishermen have begun fishing in the high seas of the Mediterranean. During the past ten years, Greece also has an aquaculture industry. Many types of fish are bred and raised on fish farms, much as land farms raise livestock for meat.

(left) A woman sells sponges in the Old Town section of Rhodes. Sponges live in colonies just off the coasts of the Greek islands. Sponge fishing created a huge export for Greece until the manufacture of artificial sponges.

(above) Fishermen tend to their boats and nets in a harbor on Thassos, an island in the northern Aegean Sea.

Farms and trees

Greece is so mountainous, and the soil is so rocky and shallow, that only one-third of the land is farmed. Many of these **cultivated** areas have little rainfall, and the soil is thin and badly eroded. Few large forests are left in Greece today, and forestry plays a small role in the country's economy.

A patchwork of tiny farms

Imagine living on a farm that has been passed down from parents to children for many generations. What started out as a large piece of land is divided equally among all the children, who in turn divide their land equally among their children, until only little plots of land are left. Some Greek farms are so small that they do not make very much money. Small farms let Greek farmers form **cooperatives** to market their crops and provide loans to farmers.

Today, more farms are growing organic produce and marketing it throughout Europe. Agritourism is another way small farmers are making money in Greece. Agritourism encourages tourists to stay on farms and learn how they operate.

Grapes and Wine

Viniculture, the tradition of growing grapes for wine, dates back to 3000 B.C. Until recently, Greek wines were sold only in Greece. Today, they are being bottled for export to other parts of the world, where they are known for their flavor and quality. The resin, or *retsina*, that Greeks often add to wine gives it a unique taste.

Farming in Greece is a mixture of old and new. Most farms are family-owned.

25

(above) Some of the world's finest olive oil is made from Greek olives.

(top) Sheep's milk is used to make cheese.

Olives: an ancient fruit

Olives and olive oil have been an important part of the Greek diet since ancient times. Olive trees are so abundant in southern and central Greece that growers cannot find enough workers to harvest the groves. Many students are hired at harvest time or workers come from Turkey. They beat the trees to bring down the olives, which are pressed to extract the oil.

Cotton, tobacco, and other crops

Cotton is an important crop for export. It is also the basis of Greece's textile industry. More than half of Greece's cotton crop grows in Thessaly, which is also known for its olives.

The Yellow Plain on the Greek mainland provides perfect conditions for vast fields of tobacco. The sale of tobacco to other countries is important for the Greek economy. Citrus fruits are also exported to European countries where it is too cold for oranges and lemons to grow. Other important crops include grains, such as wheat and barley. Rice is grown in some of Greece's river deltas.

A man herds his goats on the island of Crete. Goats are numerous in the rocky pastures and hilly regions of Greece.

Livestock

Flocks of sheep and goats are a common sight in Greece. They graze in the rocky pastures on both the mainland and the islands. These animals are raised for their milk and meat. Many Greek dishes use lamb, goat, and feta, a tasty goat milk cheese. Cattle, poultry, pigs, and rabbits are also raised.

Forest lands

Compared to agriculture and manufacturing, the forest industry plays a minor role in Greece's economy. Most of the evergreen forests that once covered much of the land have been destroyed in southern Greece. Because they are difficult to reach, the high mountains of northern Greece are still covered with forests. Trees are being planted in deforested areas to stop soil erosion and to provide much needed lumber for the building business.

Where have all the forests gone?

About 8,000 years ago, much of Greece was covered with thick forests. As more people moved into the region, the forests began to disappear. Over centuries, trees were cut down for shipbuilding and farmland, and grazing goats destroyed new growth in the forests. By the fourth century B.C., the Greek philosopher Plato was worried about the cutting down of trees on the hills surrounding Athens.

Today, Greece's forests are still threatened by human development. Each summer, fires destroy large portions of Greek forests and add to the country's air pollution problem. Many of these fires are started by developers, clearing land for construction. Deliberately set fires on the island of Sámos, in the northeast Aegean, have wiped out one-third of the pine forests and century-old olive groves.

As long as they are not trying to get to or from work, most Greeks have a relaxed attitude toward travel around the mainland and the islands. Large families and groups of friends may travel together, and the trip often turns into a social event with music, food, and fun! Sooner or later, they will get to where they are going, but getting there is half the fun.

Island hopping

An extensive ferry service of large, modern ships carries people who have patience and time on their hands to most of the islands. Ferries run frequently among the larger islands during the summer. Schedules may change at the last moment and some of the smaller islands can be reached only a few times a week. Bad weather may also keep people stranded while they wait for the wind to calm down. Some people prefer traveling by hydrofoil, a craft that skims across water. Called Flying Dolphins, hydrofoils go twice as fast as ferries but cost more.

Service can be uncertain because they do not operate in rough seas. Even on a calm day, passengers should expect a bumpy ride!

By car

Greek drivers tend to view traffic signs and signals as things to consider but not necessarily obey. This fact helps explain why Greece competes with Portugal as the country with the highest accident rate in all of Europe. Drivers going uphill almost always claim the right of way, regardless of how an intersection may be marked. Railroad crossings are rarely marked at all.

A herd of goats creates a traffic jam on a road on the island of Crete.

Greece has only a few expressways. It has many paved highways, but these can unexpectedly turn into dirt roads. In the mountain areas, these roads can be narrow and winding. In the countryside, donkeys and flocks of sheep often compete with cars for room on the road.

By rail

The major Greek railroad, OSE (Hellenic Railways Organization), connects Athens to most major cities. The Greek railway system is neither the fastest nor the most reliable way of getting around the country. Rail lines are limited to the mainland and do not extend to the west coast. Most trains run slowly, and people find buses more convenient for getting from city to city. Athens has a growing subway system, but its expansion is often stalled when workers run across ancient ruins buried beneath the city.

Taxis and buses

Buses are a popular means of travel, and a group of bus companies provides inexpensive and dependable service, even to remote places. Many buses are owned by their drivers and are decorated to reflect each owner's tastes. Taxi drivers charge each fare individually and often pick up as many people as will fit into the taxi.

(above) A map shows routes outside a subway station in Athens.

(below) Taxis and buses compete for fares in Athens.

29

(above) Deadly fires destroyed forests and homes in Greece in 2007.

(below) Scientists are trying to rescue ancient buildings from the effects of pollution.

Greece has nine national parks, home to wolves, foxes, hares, wild boars, bears, a rare species of white goat found on Crete, and 358 species of birds. Zagorochória, a region in the province of Epirus, provides a haven for rare chamois, lynx, eagles, and hawks.

Endangered pelicans

The Evros River delta, in Thrace, is a major sanctuary for endangered waterfowl. In the north, the Préspa Lakes are nesting grounds for the Dalmatian pelican and the wild pelican, both on the endangered species list. The Greek government has created a national bird sanctuary at these lakes.

Urban pollution

Big cities mean cars and factories, and these mean air pollution. In Athens and other cities, people with breathing problems are often told not to go outside in the summer. Acid rain and air pollution are destroying Greece's ancient marble monuments. Scientists have developed chemicals that soak into the stone surfaces of statues and temples and glue them together. The mixture does not stick well to marble and must be reapplied every few years. Scientists fear that continuously using chemicals may damage the ancient buildings and do more harm than good.

Fires

For years, fires were set in Greece to clear countrysides to build homes. In 2007, a number of out of control fires killed more than 60 people. The Greek government is trying to prevent more fires from deliberately being set by enforcing laws that do not allow building on land cleared by fires.

Glossary

archaeological Relating to the study of the ancient past, and the scholars, called archaeologists, who dig up the past

architecture The design of buildings

assassinate To kill a prominent person

astronomy The scientific study of space

cavalry A group of mounted soldiers

cooperative A group that bands together for a common good or cause

cultivated Prepared and used for growing vegetables, fruits, flowers, or other crops

element A substance that cannot be broken down into smaller parts by chemical means

export To send goods to other countries to be sold or traded

independent Not controlled by others

inhabitants People who live in an area

peninsula An area of land that juts out and is surrounded by water

philosopher A person who studies and thinks about ways of knowing

taverna A restaurant

textile A fabric or type of cloth

Turkish bath A place where people go to take a steam bath

Index